APOSTROPHES VI: open the grass

APOSTROPHES VI

open the grass

E.D. Blodgett

The University of Alberta Press

Published by
The University of Alberta Press
Ring House 2
Edmonton, Alberta, Canada T6G 2E1

Copyright © 2004 E.D. Blodgett
A volume in *(cuRRents)*, a Canadian
literature Series. Jonathan Hart, series editor.

Library and Archives Canada Cataloguing
in Publication

Blodgett, E. D. (Edward Dickinson), 1935-
   Apostrophes VI : open the grass /
   E.D. Blodgett.

Poems.
ISBN 0-88864-420-5

   I. Title. II. Title: Open the grass.
PS8553.L56A666 2004   C811'.54   C2004-904001-4

Printed and bound in Canada by
Houghton Boston Printers, Saskatoon
First edition, first printing, 2004
All rights reserved.

No part of this publication may be produced, stored in a retrieval system, or transmitted in any forms or by any means, electronic, mechanical, photocopying, recording, or otherwise, without the prior written consent of the copyright owner or a licence from The Canadian Copyright Licensing Agency (Access Copyright). For an Access Copyright license, visit www.accesscopyright.ca or call toll free: 1-800-893-5777.

The University of Alberta Press is committed to protecting our natural environment. As part of our efforts, this book is printed on New Leaf Paper: it contains 100% post-consumer recycled fibres and is acid- and chlorine-free.

The University of Alberta Press gratefully acknowledges the support received for its publishing program from The Canada Council for the Arts. The University of Alberta Press also gratefully acknowledges the financial support of the Government of Canada through the Book Publishing Industry Development Program (BPIDP) and from the Alberta Foundation for the Arts for its publishing activities.

 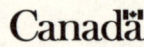

Das Gräslein ist ein Buch, suchst du es aufzuschliessen,
Du kannst die Schöpfung draus und alle Weisheit wissen.

—DANIEL CZEPKO

Tibi

Contents

1 Game	24 Father	48 Geese
2 Residence	26 Gone	49 Blind Boy
3 Flowered	27 Consequences	50 Leaving Morocco
4 Muse	28 Rites	51 Place
5 Dharma	29 Shore	52 Abandon
6 Calling	31 Fragments	53 Letter
7 Sunrise	32 Cries	54 Miracles
8 Homing	33 Grief	55 Shadowing
9 *Sotto Voce*	34 Flower	56 Coyotes
10 Asleep	35 Suspense	57 Silences
12 Across	36 Turning	58 Family
13 Angel Music	37 As If	59 Lotus
14 Epiphanies	38 Spring	60 Transfigured
15 Frogs	39 Echoes	61 Naming
16 Antiphonaries	40 Translated	62 Illumined
17 Wedding Song	41 Surrender	63 Children
18 Touching	42 Paradise	64 Yard
19 Moons	43 Tides	65 Fence
20 Equinox	44 You	66 Alphabet
21 Chiaroscuro	45 Saints	67 Visit
22 Eye	46 Recalled	68 Other Acacias
23 Gathered	47 Lindens	69 Laughter

The world that I want is nowhere—not upon the sea, nor is
it hidden in the moon, departures of the birds at twilight, nor
voices of children calling through the darkness—nowhere but where you
might be, a lift of light when you might leave a room, an echo that
cannot be placed. I thought it was a child's game that when it reached
an end would open into all that was unknown, and we would be
discovered to ourselves, the who that we had been but suddenly

a you and me that somehow were unlike, not fleshed but hidden in
a further darkness where the children were not heard, a darkness where
the absence we had thought was what the silence was could move through all
the pitches we were able to take in, and silence sang as you might sing,
your eyes in rapture gazing through the world, and in them not the rose
but what there is of roses in their mystery about to be
uncovered: silence falls so slowly from your eyes it could be held,

autumnal silences that are so distant in the air they would
not be for us to hear, but they are in you, songs that come from where
you are, that country that I am unable to attain, and when
they reach the surface of your eyes, they float abandoned there, and what
I hear as silence is the drift apart that they contain, and we
are nothing other than the child that we think that we are not
that sings to us, our bones unseen a music passing through our eyes.

Game

Your eyes were closed: horizons of the moon were neither here nor there,
and palpabilities of trees had fallen from your hands, the grass
a sharper sound beneath the wind. What residence is yours inside the dark
whose everywhere is now within your bones, your nearest neighbour next
to me, that leaves the three of us with nothing more to do but rest
together where the darkness lay upon us, blanketing the stars?
We did not know that darkness was where light arose, but we recalled

how light, wherever something was, was shadowed, light that was by darkness
plumbed. We did not know that darkness enters us in layers, light
but deeper, more unfathomable when it rests in what we thought
were our bones alone. We did not know that our origin
is darkness where inside it light is sleeping, galaxies about
to leap into the fire, our bodies what we did not know,
their brooding full of other stars that wait upon the fall of night to burn.

Residence

Where you passed by, the birds as one fell silent. All the trees, from branch
to branch were filled with them, their eyes grown bright, the trees illumined with
the light of smaller suns that gaze upon each other, knowing what
the sun has known from what it was forever, all their knowing grasped
with no more effort than an eye that opens and beholds a world all
at once, from that first moment when a god became a flower in
the emptiness of everything, a flower that sprang open, speaking

in the place where nothing heard what had been said, the sound of what
was said in his becoming flower, falling through the absent place
of everywhere, a primal rain of all about to be—stars and moon,
whatever was at first a word and now in its immensity
is mute—of stars, the moon, and hands that rest upon the silence of
your lap, around them rain that no one hears, and there are birds whose eyes
never close, in them a world where a music flowers stars.

Flowered

You sit alone inside a room. Around you are no walls but those
eternity has made. The light of stars is all you breathe, and when
you speak, it is not air that issues forth but light that takes the shape
of words, and each is so translucent you might move your fingers through
them—bright anaphoras of what you are that float around your face,
their contours yours. They rise and fall at random, you in aspects that
possess a sense you cannot grasp before they disappear and are

replaced. The only darkness visible is where your breath is spaced
by what you say, and if there is desire in eternity,
it is desire for the dark refusing to be word, and so
eternity has unsuspected endings, all the dark that seeps
inside your words and takes up residence at last inside your breath:
you cannot speak the dark, but it speaks you in echo, echo of
the you that you are not, that other breath that says what you would say.

Muse

It seemed as if the snow that lay upon the branches had been there
forever, and the light surrounding them the absolute of blue
that was their shape in echo. Of the trees the only memory
is where the snow returns in us, a snow that is the shape of what
we know, the light inside us and the snow the blue where branches and
the burden that they bear against the sky is open, all that they
have been imprinted there. Perhaps it is that no one is recalled

by anyone as what they might have been, unable in the air
to find where they had been, except as something that might fall into
the eye at random, quickly taking shape. You might say O, and in
that moment, that circumference the what of it is taken, whole,
unable to be lost. But what in you is that completion, utter
knowing of the snow, the trees, the shape they take inside the light?
No one knows who we have been unless as snow we fall through that

remembering embrace of air, the place where we have been and then
are not, the our that we knew given again a figure that
we were unable to perceive ourselves, to be a tree that holds
the snow, around us that recalling O without awareness of
itself, an O that is the echo of another sphere where stars
are in their light with no distinctions of the night and day—*there*
we are, another absolute of blue that keeps the tree and snow.

Dharma

The moon rises in the mind, everything ceding in its passage,
all the stars around it fired in the thought of it, a sky
unable to recall the darkness but as dark dissolving in
the presence of the moon and other light the wake of it: no
one thinks the stars are more than silence in their sky, but these are stars
that when the moon appears, make music that cannot be heard—it falls
as rain invisible, and all the air awake, its wakefulness

the music that we had forgot, the only silence darkness gone.
So the stars, and what the moon is is you, the place where music
turns toward in its emergence from the dark, and in its turn
the time it keeps is given to it by the moon that is not known
but in the music that is nowhere it is not. I cannot say
that I possess my mind, and if it is, it is in music, a
refrain of stars that has no other calling but to utter moon.

Calling

We were walking in the sun, horizons everywhere beneath
our feet: I heard you speak, and it was not words that came from your mouth,
but what you said was standing bright before your eyes, nothing that had
more sound than grass might have beneath a windless sky, speaking at first
of what you were when you were in your childhood, and it was not
a child that we saw, but joy stood there upon its toes, beside
it sudden sorrow, afternoons that never seemed to end, the sense

of something that cannot, a shadow of a bird with wings that do
not move, and all of them together strung upon the air in sighs
of syllables of their desire, each a sentence that poured forth
into our eyes with no shade of meaning falling to explain
their being in the air. What did I say but something of the glass
that always stood between the world and me, of trees and how they rose
inside the glass, their presence in the world lifted into light?

And so they were again before us—trees of glass and shadows of
infinities of afternoons—the breath that issued from our mouths
inaudible but absolutely shaped, our words more than shapes:
this is how *fiats* leap into the space that planets keep,
and moons turn, suspended always on our breath, another breath
inside it coming from the centre of the sun where silence is
its radius, and our voices the circumference in fire.

Sunrise

Birds were floating through your body, nesting in your heart, akin
to birds that I had seen above the towns of childhood, the light
grown dim above the hush of trees, a winter dusk that slipped into
my bones till I was chilled, a naked boy upon a naked plain,
immensity the only home in sight, but all the birds that found
their way into your body one by one became invisible,
barely to be heard as voices that rise up inside your voice,

the burdens that they bear of memories of air and sky when they
descended through their emptiness and stood upon your heart: for them
it was a coming back to somewhere they had never been, unknown
but known, the place that came upon them in their dreams when they would dream
of where beginnings are, and what they sang of I had heard before,
but farther in the evening where they disappeared, their singing now
as soft, and turning on the silence where one gathers breath at first.

Homing

You were watching children passing by the house, the little group
amorphous as it paused and circled, then moved on at random, its
shape a kind of cloud apart from other clouds and moving through
from nowhere into nowhere under its own wind, your eyes drawing
down upon them in a silence that recalled the silence of
a tree that fills with birds arriving unperceived—in our minds
before becoming birds—and I was standing by your side, my eyes

upon your thoughts as they would form upon your face, another dance
upon another landscape in the twilight, thoughts that were the sounds
of other birds, of pigeons after rain upon a distant roof,
the murmurs that they make almost inaudible so that we hear
them but without our knowing that we hear: they hid beneath your eyes,
only to reappear beside your mouth, assuming shapes that might
have been a smile, but fleeting, thoughts that seemed to cover other thoughts

that would not be revealed, their shyness that of children that are deep
inside whatever in the world they appear to do, their play
the shape of what they are, their bodies the intent of what is in
their mind, but an intent they share, a dancing mind of bodies that
passes into the light between your eyes and where they come again
long after they have gone as music we remember, music or
a rain that stops farther away, not known, but somewhere in the air.

Sotto Voce

The world lay asleep within my ear, only its breathing to
be heard, and there lay tragedy and planets and the cries of birds
that used to pierce the day, whatever is was there where it had found
a place to fall, each one a ruin in the shape of children sleeping
there, and you and I, who are the world too, picked carefully
a way among them, all consumed in merely taking in their breaths

and letting them depart into the night that lay upon them in
their absolute surrender. When you spoke to call upon me, all
the words that you were saying wound into their breathing—so it was
impossible for me to get the sense, but only notes across
the breathing air. I said that we could not be lost, this was the world,
and we were in it, all of it, there was no other place to go,

Asleep

and when it woke, it would be death awake that was a child here,
and nothing would illuminate the change, the unremitting dirges
of the trees that wake to find themselves alone upon the margins
of the skies, the wind gone, and silence rising in the space
that they had held, their silence then within my ear, silence and
the memory of breathing through the night, no other voice but yours

that floats across it calling through the dark. Perhaps our only life
is when we are completely given up to sleep, and fallen and
as children are, our mother but the air, all that we are the draft
and giving up of what we have been given to take in, the rest
the loss of our abandon, waking into trees that rise, but rise
to disappear, a wake of children crying out among the leaves.

I have given up apocalypse—we are already on
the other shore where day and night do not stand opposite each other
and the moon is always in the morning sky, the stars beside
it brilliant as the sun, and where we thought it was an apple tree
in flower, it was you, and all the bees around you smaller stars,
their fire not a fire we recalled, but fire that contained
a universe in alphabets unknown to us, and everything

that was to be already spelled but still without the shape that seeing
needs, its knowledge given us without the space that falls between
the thing that rises up before our eyes and its becoming an
idea, all of it inside us and complete, and we were nought
but places of a larger affirmation where a world lay
already formed in that shape their *fiat* would assume when it
unveiled sprang spoken into air, the sound of its beginning gone.

Across

An O upon the surface of the sea! and through the opening
the fish could gaze beyond the canopy of heaven that they knew
to watch the suns go by and stars in their lucidity at night
appear, the empyrean given over to their wonder. You
and I were walking close to where the sea was lapping at our feet,
and through the opening the O had made the docile schools of fish
came into view, unmoving in the newness of the sudden light—
we must have been within their deepest contemplation, angels that

could bear the thinnest air, unscathed by bright proximities of fire.
An awe rose up from the silence of the sea beyond the heaven of
its shores that was not heard by us but by the birds that filled what we
beheld as heaven, and the music that descended over us
was music that was made of silence and of fire, its burden O,
an O that echoes through the elements till it becomes a sleeve
that fits around our flesh, the limits that we bear uncertain in
the light, a universe afloat, the surface of the sea dissolved.

Angel Music

For you there was not anything that did not hold epiphany,
the smallest flower capable, a drop of water rain had left
upon a cup of leaf, a footstep that remained behind, the shape
of hands upon a wall, their shadows mimics of a universe—
or is that all that anyone can be, nothing they see but what
they are in what stands up beside them unadorned? Then you, that I
would summon now in these barest words, you would be there, and not bereft
of anything, and certain instants of the light which starts from where

you would not think it possible, from deep within the ground to well
up in the air and overcoming sun and moon, a fountain of
the light that stands beside the things that are the world, of light that were
it possible would speak, the history of things that are laid bare
and each of them becoming known as what they are. Then you would be
within that fountain, gestures of your knowledge rising up above,
the summons of your hands a world flowing over you, and we
the everything that you behold, disclosed in your eternity.

Epiphanies

Before we were to fall asleep, the music of the singing frogs
rose up above the marshes, over the grass and settled near us in
the room where we lay gazing at the air above us filling with the song
they made, its cadences a pulse of earth released and given to
the air: there are no angels that could utter all the joy that filled
the twilit air that moved around, and as we gazed, the walls that framed
our house became the air, and we were not reclined upon a bed

but what they sang of moved beneath us, all our sense of gravity
in what they said, untranslatable as grass and flesh but all
of it, the silence and the sound exhaled, was known, as we would know
a moon that we had never seen, whose light descends across the dark
and stays where we would stay, an intimate that we take in without
a word exchanged, our only house this knowing that suddenly comes
for just a moment out of emptiness inhaled, the music ours.

Frogs

. Trees have other majesties: in their effulgent summers they
alone define the sky, the clouds their echo, mute between the leaves,
but you, closer to the earth than they, their one desire to
attain the sun, their leaves the wings of great birds that are bereft,
unable to depart, but you, when you are standing in their midst
give up to them the light they cannot reach, but light that comes upon
them from beneath, and they are taken by surprise, the shade that held

the sun returned wherever it comes down across your flesh, and you
by moments are for them a moon that rises in the dark that they
have shed, and all around them motions of the sea rise up and fall,
their leaves the sea's antiphonary that in silence answers, rising
toward the sun and falling toward the sea that follows you, the pace
it takes never uncertain but in measures that are not within
a range we know, larger and larger where the trees encompass us.

Antiphonaries

Some journeys never end—they seem to move and not to move, their pace
a sea that splashes up and down the shore where all the stones
are daily lost from sight to reappear unchanged and polished more
brightly than they were remembered, the sea a surface that for them
is breath that in their centuries of rolling on the coast lays down
upon them what they will return of light, and in this journey you
are moved to be, unable to turn back, a journey that is not

the sea and not the stones that it possesses in its movement, but
the air infinity alone exhales, that moves in you when you
are you, the sea upon you and the light of stones that see! returns,
a light that has no place to go but round itself, forever growing
larger as the stone it was recedes beneath the sea, a light
that is an aura of the infinite distilled, and you inside
it going round, another sphere of music and the sea and stones,

rondeau of what but seems to be in sight, the shape of it without
an outline, air that were it visible would be of everything
that in its gravity is held to turn upon itself unbidden,
endless and complete, and from its rising up the singing of
the visible invisible forever rounded off, its sense
coming and going in the larger reaches of the light that turns
upon the sea expanding through the last horizon of the air.

Wedding Song

Nothing lay before you on the ground, and you were singing to
yourself a song unknown to me, the music of it coming from
you everywhere, your flesh the instrument it played upon, and what
you sang fell out upon the air and settled where the nothing that
was on the ground stood up and danced, a silent dance of nothing, air
and what there was of flesh made music—from your fingers flowers grew,
and nothing stood around you, nothing of blue and yellow, you inside

the flowers that we saw, their evanescence nothing without you
who sit upon the doorstep of infinity, the dance that you
are moving in the dance that makes of us in our brevity
a dance where suns leap up from darkness pausing on your hands, its light
a dance of nothing but largesse that is a universe where you,
the singing centre of what is in passing, are, invisible
inside the dance, and turning all that we in our moments touch.

Touching

There is a space that falls between the night and day, and in the space
a dog is sitting, staring into what cannot be seen before
the light appears—from time to time it barks, and when the silence follows
after, it is silence that fills up with solitude, each
time a separate solitude that echoes over night and day,
each illumined by a little moon before it takes its shape,
and walking through a garden of such little moons, you in your

beginnings came, no more than intimations in the air of night
and day, an echo on the mind's horizon walking in and out,
where nothing can be grasped, no more than any moon that brings to us
the light of silence, solitude before it is a solitude
awake within the deepest dream of wakefulness, and all that you
could be was hesitation, only space that was not night or day,
an uninvented word that waits upon the coming of the world.

Moons

A line was drawn across the sky, a line that was composed of birds
that were about to merge a season with another, endings and
beginnings taking one design: snow is possible upon
the sun, and we are now by ourselves within the shadow of
the birds that make a line against the sky, a we that is of light
and dark, the edges of us more of air than flesh and so where birds
take flight, unknowing yet of what their path should be, but motion poised,

a tree that is the certainty of our horizon suddenly
might disappear, drawn up into the wake of the invisible
behind the passing birds, and you will say it is autumnal mist,
its leaves are lying at our feet, the memory of its rising ours.
When everything is gone, we will be the sky where it resumes
and nothing else—from it the snow will fall and suns through emptiness
pour out, birds will be heard where they have been, the sky their song.

Equinox

Sunsets lingered in your hair beneath the gathering birds and we
could sense the presence of the stars above them all, invisible
but bright beyond the falling sun, the darkness that had not yet come
a darkness that was always covered with a light it cannot take,
and we have no more power than the dark that moves around us in
the way the tides upon a shore will move, a dark incapable
of more than random sloping through the night. But birds, you say, the birds

are darkness springing with desire, another dark inside the dark
that moves it up against the light and then away, a dark that knows,
bearing the shade apart. But birds, wherever they may go, go longingly
beneath the light, the stars upon their backs, the burdens that they bear
ineffable and bright, unable to elude the radiance
that always in their distances endures, and birds remember nothing
nor the stars, the nothing they remember weaving dark unthinking

through the air around your head. Of all that lasts it is the light,
and so your hair is where the sun lies down to sleep beneath the stars
and floating birds that rise and fall upon the light, and if your hair
should dream, its dream would be of light that falls and falls, its falling what
there is of universes, the huge air that stands above the seas,
the space we think is sky, its light falling through distances beyond
the sun, all the knowing we can have and given up to birds.

Chiaroscuro

Your eye is where the world gathers shape, a deer that looks across
a field at you, the sun that disappears behind its back, a deer
becoming silhouette, and trees, and smaller hills behind that lose
their undulations as the day grows late, the light draining away:
where is the world is what your eye is asking, moving through the fading
day, where is the sun, now that darkness has appeared, the stars
apart, their little light unable to bring us the deer that we

were sure was near, the trees that never go away, where is the world
but known in that unhesitant departure, rising with stars,
there where your eye in its dispersals wanders over grass in its
abandonment, a grass that now invisible you want to know
beneath your hands, a grass to rise in memory when all the light
is gone, a grass ungraspable, its patience all that it can give,
where you lie down your body handed over to the giving up?

Eye

Standing in the autumn light, we thought we gathered apples as
they fell beneath the tree, and while they fell we looked deeper into
the air that was the place of their finalities, briefly passing
through the air to settle for a moment on the grass, and deep
within the air our eyes went on, the apples giving us a kind
of music that fell farther in the distance after us, unable
to keep up, their falling silence falling, filling all the air

around us with a music no more audible than people walking
on horizons where our eyes where drawn, people that were seen
to stand against the sun, their merest outlines almost spread across
the remnants of the light, the evening what they were, and as we looked,
the apples fell from us to disappear into the night within
the grass, where music, apples and the passing silence held us, no
way out, no difference between the distance and the grass beneath.

Gathered

I think of you as stones that one might see along a beach at dusk.
They are incapable of sound, the silence that they harbour all
that they can be. The water of the sea from time to time washes
over them and they awaken, rattling against themselves,
their silence turned to emptiness that falls through emptiness. It is
a sound that does not seem to come from where the stones are lying
but from distances that slowly shift inside eternity.
If ruins spoke, this would be their message, randomly evoked,
the sea caressing earth with rapid passages of laughter given

to the sand, the fitful air, and if there were no moon, they would
not be perceptible but as the way that absence takes one by
surprise, an absence that had never gone away, familiar
when heard as old refrains from which the words have disappeared. The scene
beneath the moon has pliant edges. Who would think how adamant
it is, the sea that always falls upon the shore, the stones that bear
it, music that cannot be music, only water running out
into itself across the stones? If they could hear, it would be music
from the moon that entered them, carrying the sea across

Father

their thinning stoniness. These are stones that taught me how to cry,
the water welling up unbidden from a sea that in me moved
and moving flowed against the only shore that it might know, a sea
that summoned forth from them no audible reply where they lay helpless
as the sea came down. I did not seem to be the I I knew—
a newly risen moon, perhaps, that gazes with a new surprise
upon the sea and stones that lie beneath and knows them as the scope
of its domain, darkness ebbing in its wake, darkness of stones
that lie untouched but held within the light, abandoned to the sea.

Night was lying on the floor beside us and without a moon
you might have said that it had entered through the windows, spread itself
from wall to wall, and died, inside it all the stars and what we could
remember of the moon. The words that we had spoken lay beneath
it unretrievable. We are without cover, the universe
without the shape that had conferred a sense on what we said, able
to say *moon* and know what followed—infinite surprise that then

arose and seemed to say what we could not. And now without it we
are nothing but ourselves, the night unmoving at our feet, reduced
to finding alphabets within the dark that must replace what we
had thought the stars to be. We hear a sound that moves across the dead
of night, uncertain who had made it, a beginning that is like
an O, but longer, an unbroken *o* that is not our speech
but something shaped to take us in, around us and inside us, air

that touches us, and given into our hands to keep, the shape
of what we are when other shapes are gone, but neither you nor I
possess it, we reside inside it, all possession of ourselves
the thing we lost when our words had disappeared within the night,
and now what knowledge of ourselves that we might have starts there in what
we hear, but hearing it with our bodies held inside it, moons
and night unnecessary, all the loss they hold for us dispelled.

Gone

And so, what can the moon be, and who are we? We must be
the place where waiting enters, taking root, and if it flowers, it
would take the shape of waiting, upon a ground of stones, over them
the space where moons before had moved, the air infinity that now
inhabits us. The life that we are summoned to take on can only
happen here, the flowers that are given us the flowers that have made
of us the barest of containers, holding them. The memory

of stones is now the memory that enters us, a memory
that only knows the intricate designs that waiting has, a waiting
that is only what can be remembered, memories of endless
rains that washed them through the centuries, the rains of what they are:
the waiting that possesses stones is fullness without measure, it
cannot imagine any consequence, the memory of stones
the pure rotundity of our sphere that turns upon itself.

Consequences

The sea is never still, lying before us at the close of day,
and scattered over it the moon comes down in pieces dancing on
its surface, little gestures of the light upon the dark, and you
might say there is a tree that stands beyond our sight that sheds its leaves
at night across the world, leaves that do not come to light before
they strike the darkness of the sea beneath to rest upon it till
they disappear when morning comes. I have seen you walk along

the edge of oceans, kneeling near to gather in what falls as night
through all its watches turns, no more companions than the moon
and stars, your body bent upon the water lifting light, around
you autumn offered through the moon. No one can say what this is for,
or where the light is put away and garnered, holding more than merely
moon, but fragments of a universe that gives itself in light
departing into air, a gift of disappearance through itself.

Rites

A single flock of birds went by above the sea, and nothing came
behind: the moon remained, and underneath its light the sea revealed
itself, its infinite expanse within a light that did not seem
to radiate, but merely be, a light whose absence could not be
conceived. I heard you speak, and all you said was 'O,' a naked O
that floated from your mouth and paused upon the light. It seemed to be
an answer, but it was not certain what it was that summoned it,

but when it came, we knew that something was complete, and if the birds
returned, they would be new, their coming and their going rhythms that
were not their own but of the light, its breath above the sea, the only
o that it might utter. Where do endings enter here in this
infinity? Wherever you might look, the distance empties, in
it falls the moon, the open sea, the line that seemed to be the shore
a line where nothing follows, oceans breathing there the falling moon,

and if the sea, then we must be revealed, and apples, summer, snow
beneath the moon, and each of us in motion going nowhere, the
steps we take returning steps of our infinity: so snow
suddenly fills the air among the ripened apples, summer on
our shoulders. What can we recall that is not all about us, an
insistence in the air that is of now, the snow among the apples
every snow? And you a child, dreams unfolding in your sleep,

Shore

where you are in the summers that have gone? We are what wakens in
us, summer or the snow in their perfections—*they* remember us,
without them sleep would lay upon us, closed in our wordless flesh,
the moon unknown to us, and we stand up in their returns, their
proximity what we have thought to be the emptiness of air, the what
that we are given, that remembered I that is in you, is given
instantly, a voice that echoes in the ripeness here, beside.

When I die, before the darkness oozes through the universe,
I pray that then there will be words to find you as you are and not
as I have dreamed you in these fragments that can be nothing more
than rapid passages of light that leap apart from what must be
the greater fire to disappear unnoticed in the air, as you
might see a leaf descend through autumn light and for a moment
seem to be the light more brightly lit and not a leaf, the tree
from which it fell unseen in its illumination, overcome

with silence, moving air, the light. But silence is a sea abandoned
to the moon that moves upon us in the longer light of afternoons,
a sea that is a figure of infinity, the moments of its shores
unmeasured, dancing waves its only place, and we are how their rise
and fall occur, the silence of it our shape invisible:
your hand is moving now in air, and now is sleeping at your side,
your breath a tidal change, a dance that has no name, but is the dance
that silence seeks, impossible to hold, its turning everywhere.

Fragments

You cry at night. It breaks the dark, and pieces of it fall about
us, lying in the air invisible, their presence everywhere.
The cries are brief, mere punctuations of the silence that contains us: when
they pass, it is a world that has passed, not just the house, the tree
beside the window, garden, grass, a world where all that is left
is echoes of your cries, and with them we are gone, no one to
remember what it was. Perhaps it is a dream, a dream that I,

not you, have had, for in our waking nothing stands before you saying
what it was, but what they were is everywhere, the pitch of that
irrevocable loss that moves through us, a sea withdrawing that
cannot return, and with it shores and what we might recall of shores,
even the air grown empty. Now there are no borders, where we might
decide to place our hands recedes before us, the sun falling so
far westward that the west is gone from sight, your tears the only stars.

Cries

Grief is a certain colour that has not been named. It does not come
at times we most expect it, when the sun has disappeared or late
in autumn moving through the naked trees. Grief is never a
surprise, but comes with more familiarity than any friend
possesses, taking our hands in hers, and once arrived she stays
with us at home, invisible but our dark anatomy
who dances us unknowing on the grass. Grief is not the last

farewell, it is the first, beside us from the moment our eyes
are filled with light that we have never seen before—then we know
the sum of all we need to know, the shadow that we carry with
us in the world. Sunlight falls upon your hand, and as it moves
to take it in, the grief that lies unseen within you is what moves,
to have the light once more pervading you. Grief is not the giving
up, it is the spring of our desire, always to be both now and then,

the dance we know we are unending, its beginning when the stars
begin. What greater grief is there but not to have grief take up
its residence inside our bones, to be the silence that we think
is ours, the silence that is but the breath of music rising in
the dance of our breath? What is our cry but grief that is
the one embrace we have for night, the stars we cannot see, the we
we cannot be that we have left somewhere forgotten, taken away.

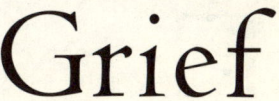

Of all the gestures this one—when you place a flower in a vase,
you linger, holding it above the water for a moment, placing it
in air where it is all alone, and gathering the solitude
of other flowers into it—of all the gestures this one takes
you into that flower of solitude, alone with air and moments
that expand, everywhere a world held in what you have done:
the birds that pass across the sky descend and stop in flight, unable

to discover what eternity has fallen over them, their song
suspended, what they had been singing now forgotten, but the note
is what possessed the world, no place to go but to horizons of
that sound, a note that is the voice that solitude must have when it
has nothing other than a flowering of solitude in which
to be, and there we are, our voices not to be distinguished from
that song that never ends, but hovers near, a flower in your hand.

Flower

If the sea would sleep, its sleep would be inside you, stars
at rest upon your hands. We can be no more full than this, and no
more without grasp upon the world—children, then, but children in
their fullness, flesh made light. The world is not spread out before our eyes,
the streams that we remember flowing farther from us, but behind
them, trees that stood unchanged upon the ground that we provide. Nothing
else is ours, and so we are as people sitting on the air,
and everything around us held suspended in the gravity

where we are also held, the breath that we hold breathless ours while
it stays with us, a gift in passing. What have we to give but ground
that given stays and on it falls whatever falls—stars, seas,
air—for us to gaze in our apparent blindness on, and we
are falling always, our pace the same as theirs, unable to
hold back: *then* it is ours as we belong to it, the skin we feel
the feel of stars as they move down the sky and nothing in between,
the slow fall of children falling hidden in their gravity.

Suspense

Overhead at night, geese are softly passing, heard before
their cries cut through the night as one by one they call at intervals,
the air awake between us and the naked moon. But in their cries
nothing is no more naked than the trees that stand beneath them, their
appeal reaching toward them, memories of the sun inside them, arms
upheld, the shape that prayer takes when there is nothing left to do
but pray: beneath their summer shade we walked, and all there was of us
to see were our eyes, returned as naked offerings to the sun.

Everywhere a snow comes down, the sound of it descending through
the night, falling through the trees that rise in our nakedness,
the hush of it settling in your hand. Whatever you have held—
not roses but the air that they exhale that is a breath inside
your breath—that is the hush that rises there, the sound of it the sound
of nakedness and nothing more, every moment of a life
surrendered then, the asking that is in the light, the stance of trees,
not asking but the what of what we are, birds turning at night.

Turning

It's funny, then, that here we are, standing face to face to speak
as if it were a final time, a time apart from other times
when we had stopped and hailed each other, spoke and then went on, as if
we had not always been at sea with no idea of where the port
might be and its approaches, or if we were ever to arrive,
our compass always set for harbours that are nowhere to be seen,
and when we thought we saw the sun, it was the moon more brightly lit
and many moons in pieces floating near us in the water sending

light around, and as we passed, we spoke of Homer, say, as if
he were a friend of our youth, or Sappho, or—but nothing is
as if, it is, and that is all, the ships that we had thought were there,
the sun that was the moon, the ports that were our shared trajectories,
what can they be but how we gave the world shape the little while that we
would move beside each other, believing it was day and we could see,
but when time seems final, hypotheses begin to disappear
and we have nothing left to say but one or two farewells and then

God speed, and time to see new distances appear and harbours
looming in the dark that we had not foreseen, approaching us,
the journeys that we thought were ours theirs, giving us the routes
that we could not have known, as if we had been always sleeping, each
of us another's dream that wakes in our farewells and sees that we
are now a dream of someone else, where moons rise up in months whose names
we do not know, the shores in places we have never touched, and at
our feet seas reappear, familiar, as if not ebbing away.

As If

Spring would enter you slower than any other season of
the year, and when it came, it came as lilacs open in the air,
lilacs that were not visible to you but were what spring was full
of, purple spring that you breathed in until you were not who you were,
the child I remember, you were what the spring became, the purple
smell that was its fullness through the nights that now have gone, the streets
that are but only as they rise in memory, and you are walking
there your pace the pace infinity is moving in among the young,

remembered trees, familiar stars, your face almost unknown to me,
a crescent moon that has not seen its other phases turning in
the open sky, and if I now would call to you, you could not hear
this voice that circles round your infinite, unknowing turning through
the skies that I recall, no shadow moving where you rise: where are
you, then, and how, the moon autumnal now, are you to know that this
is what we are, unable to be where I am when you are only
childhood, its absence that will only rise against another

heaven when a cry goes up in me to summon up what I
have thought you are, a moon that does not know its fullness, lilacs a
sufficiency that never fail, nor have you words for me, your face
itself the smell that lilacs make, a face invisible as what
you breathe, the crescent moon a flower open in the springs where you
are everywhere, a voice behind a hedge that no one hears, a cry
that cannot rise beyond the infinite of where its music falls,
the sea beneath and calm, a breath of lilacs rising over it.

Spring

Sometimes there is nothing to say, and so we sit and listen to
the emptiness of air before us open randomly, the cries
of birds suddenly filling it, the silence after them a silence that
is now a silence full, a silence that has entered our time
that we can see as emptiness that has the colour blue behind
it, clouds that fill it momentarily, air remembered in
another sky, and at the same moment we hear the trees, the grass

that stands beneath us say itself, and what it says begins to enter
us, whatever was upon the threshold of our ears invisible
as stars that rise above us in the day, but when we hear them, they
resume in us, the primal call for light the summons that they send
deep in the mutest tissues of our flesh, and so we cannot speak,
the resonance their names might carry not remembered, the silence that
is on our tongues an echo of the stars that are and are not seen.

Echoes

I remember I had written ten fragments, longer than
the ones that Moses heard, that came to me as from another tongue,
and in their passage into mine the way was so slow that I
began forgetting what the words had said: what came to mind was this—
that moving from the other tongue to mine was full of detours I
had not foreseen, and all the words were clear, but put together were
impossible for me to grasp when I had woken up, and then
I saw you lying by my side, remembering that also you

are slow to wake, your hair untouched by wind, everything calm about
you, you beginning to fill the body you inhabit when you are
of us. You did not dream, you said, coming it seemed from that
uncompassed emptiness that we are in night after night, the flesh
surrounding us at ease, deserted here upon the shore of a
forgotten life, the life that we are sure is ours, certain that
the life we dream is only ours as breath, an air that enters us
invisible, our life in our flesh on hold. We touched our mouths

to reassure ourselves, our tongues seeking the light they knew
before the fall of night, and when they speak so to each other they
are wordless, silent and unable to wander away: they are,
together or apart, remembering their one life, and that they
are only children of the possible that are without a past,
their only knowledge knowledge of a moon that comes and goes, a moon
that passes through them as we breathe, a moon invisible that holds
us as we are, awake inside the self we dream, our earth the air.

Translated

We sat inside the evening. Everything around us moved and we
took note of birds in ones and twos that passed almost without a sound,
of leaves that rise and fall, the air upon their faces, murmurs of
a river somewhere nudging up against its banks, of grass that in
the growing darkness at our feet comes up inaudible, of day
departing, absence filling up with dusk. We take note of what
we think is there, unable to recount it but as sequences
of our imagining, a world standing up inside us for
the moment of its one duration, always itself amorphous where
we are, a world shaped at random that we think is ours in its
fugacity, forgetting that it is the evening that has taken

us into its endless moments of dispersal where there is
so little given us to know, our one capacity desire
to believe that as it is to us it is, and were we not
to hear the steps of children walking somewhere on the borders of
the evening where we sat, we would believe them there imperative
as grass, perhaps believing them to be as us in analogue,
not us but us in memory, an evening then inside a breath
of evening that can only come in sight without our seeing it,
an evening then of our fugacity not its, the going away
of day the going away of what we think we were, and known because
it moves without a sound, taking our desire with it, away.

Surrender

Paradise was put into your hand. It might be gone before
the dawn shall come, and so it will not be a paradise that you
have seen in books perhaps. This is a paradise where all that moves
is seen but barely—nothing then to name when everything is known
by touch—a paradise that has no story, no beginning but
of shapes that have no shape to be described, no Noah needed then
for their perpetuation: what they are is not what they have been,

their being being without. This is all the paradise that we
might wish to have, the tree, the stream, the apple, sleep, surprise and then
the gesture that could not be taken back—these are not put into
your hand, nor knowledge that you did not seek, but what you grasped without
request is the before of us, a what of us so naked that
we were without the sense of flesh to hide, possessing us as we
had been in our eternity and for a moment afterward.

Paradise

Nothing can be done about the moon, its slow arrivals and
departures through the darkness that descends upon our flesh, emblem
of inevitable order, tides inscribed upon its face,
the rhythm of the breathing earth the changing of its light: it rules,
but rules without the barest sense of what it is—mere stone, perhaps,
an afterthought that fell into the universe to move around
in circles, closed, beyond appeal. Another moon is ours, its

intransigence in us—our breath, our bones, the dance that they put down
against the ground. And if we have an origin, the moon that turns
inside the darkness of the flesh we share is where the what of what
we are begins: we are the tides of this moon, a moon rising
as a question in the mind, its answers but arrivals and
departures of the light that is the ebb and flow of both the dark
and us, our knowledge ceremonies of our farthest origins.

Tides

And so to talk with you is as one might converse with trees or ponds
whose surfaces are full of floating moons. Imagine someone passing
by and you and I in sight: what would be heard but something leaves
might say responding to the slightest breeze, or water rocking up
against a shore. But you and I are talking always, the words in us
as words that rise in dreams, become birds, and disappear as birds:
our words have no more sound than moons, no transcription near enough
to write them as they are—not words, but that unbroken being of
one mind where trees are nowhere but in that uncertain place

that seems to have no place to go, looking around only to see
where moons have been and ponds, a mind we share with them. So when
I gaze at you and you return it, I am you for you—and trees
and ponds. Here is where we all lie down together, figments of
a grander dream, our thoughts the smaller dream, our words not ours but
the singing no one hears that rises in the mind where we are thought,
the you of me remembered in a dream that you or birds might have,
carried into farther shores of light where I might wake, thinking
myself alone and floating, a rocking word of water full of moons.

You

It is not possible to gaze upon the small Peruvian town
that hangs above the bed where sunlight falls in late afternoons
across the orange coloured tiles of the roofs, the llama on
the point of going past, the woman with her bundled sticks. It is
a village somewhere high among the mountains, not a tree in sight:
how not at evening, before falling asleep, not to remember you
are dead, the little town a gift passed on from that small country where

your dreams were found, dreams of thinner air, paler skies, and words
that flustered in your ears like birds too small to see? It is the kingdom
of the dead you might have said, if you were here, where nothing moves,
the llama always ready, but unable. But with the sun upon
it fading slowly, saints are brought to mind, the kind that used to hang
above the beds of sleeping people, their protection falling through
the deeper dark that fills a room at night. From time to time the woman

with the sticks appears to smile, a smile that you must have bequeathed
to her. Recalling yours, it is a distant smile that gathers in itself
something only it has known, but this is distance all alone
that spreads across her face, a smile filled with everything thin and pale,
and in the darkness it descends on towns and llamas, mountains and
the absence of the trees. The dreams that will be dreamt beneath it rise
from such a distance asking to come in with very small hands.

Saints

The light we saw behind the birches was already gold, an early
morning light that was hardly light but light recalled, a light
unmoving in the leaves, and you might say it was as old as all
the light that sprang into the universe upon the first day
when everywhere there was no more than nothing to behold, before
the light, the dark, the waters, and the rising of the sun and moon,
the sudden grass, the trees across the new savannahs, and the seas
of whales and smaller fish, the butterflies and unfamiliar flowers

filling air, and all remembered in the light that glowed among
the birches standing in the garden, the rain that fell at night fresh
upon its leaves: if we are they, then we are who we are recalled,
the light upon our flesh as old as on the first day, or last,
the garden where we stand containing others, what we do not see—
the lions on the grass, the whales against the shores, the smallest of
the creatures hidden in the air, and sudden birds exploding from
it, shadows coming over us. Nothing remains forgotten, each

of us another held in memory. But what does light recall
if not itself, its ageing where its youth endures? So we are
our memory of us, the day creation ends the day that we
begin, the garden where we are the garden that remembers more
than gardens, memory itself in birches and the grass that bears
upon its surface every trace of every passing thing, the wind
inside the shade unseen, and our we in it invisible,
the light more golden there, the air archaic moving on our skin.

Recalled

Before we fell asleep, you sang a song that came from where you lived
when you were young, and in the song a man was standing under trees
that had just begun to flower—early summer linden trees
where bees were moving slowly through the yellow dust—and in your voice
lakes rose up and distant forests that were ancient long before
you heard them floating from another's mouth when you were young and all
the music that you breathed was laden with a purity that is

in bees, the paler green of lindens, and the song suspended in
the air between the man and someone else, a spirit barely seen
beyond the trees, and now the notes of it are falling all around
us, a rain of song that falls upon us so slowly that its pure
appeal lies down on us as palpable as any other rain,
but rain that is a memory of rain that cannot be of any
good to trees, yet in its falling something stays upon us, a

fragrance of rain that we inhale, and something more than forests—their
aurora of a time that no one now remembers—and we thought
that when we fell asleep, it was beside a lake where water from
the mountains came remembering the rain that had been sung upon
their slopes, and on the surface of the lake we saw the faces it
gave back, but faces that were not exactly ours as we had thought
they were, with lindens standing up beside them filled with singing bees.

Lindens

Sometimes when the geese are heard, gathering in the early fall,
they sound like geese that are very small and somewhere beside us in
the room, summoning us to bring to mind what we already know
and have forgotten through the shorter summer nights: we look into
each other's eyes to read ourselves, the only knowledge that we have
of seasons rising there, but when the geese call, it seems as if
our looking gathers holes, and parts of us cannot be seen with all
the clamour of the geese between, and we are somehow of the flock

but unlike them we have no wings and are unable to depart.
We are almost carried away, forgetting our summons is
the seasons we see lying in our eyes—for them summer is
the only time, an eternity that is their gift, to be
always closer to the sun, while we are always giving up
and getting back, and each time uncertain of the return, the sun
itself appearing surprised when summer happens again and brings inside
it the eternity of geese that fills our brevity once more.

Geese

You stand before us for your brief eternity, intent upon
the songs of birds that break around you in the air, invisible
to you and us, perhaps inside their forests or within the air
itself, continually flying near—and how their cries cut through
the clarity of all the skies, not one but thousands falling down
about us, skies in fragments crying out, the stars unseen but known
in each note we hear—and when they sing your fingers reach to touch
themselves, the code of what they know when they have heard it all, shattered

through the air transcribed upon your naked skin, the broken heavens
written there, and this is what you body forth, revealing it
to us in arabesques that disappear as soon as they become
what stands between the you you are and everything outside that is
not known in any other way, a sudden coming somewhere then
taken away. And so you die and die again forever, the
report of it already in the cries of birds and our eyes,
the giving and the taking of it all the life that you might know.

Blind Boy

Distance is not the space that opens up between the world, you
and me, the other stars, the moon, it is the endlessness of night
and its *askesis*, standing nowhere to be seen, but its effect
distilled upon our longing flesh—it is a hand that open holds
us, all the winds that falling from the planets touching us without
a mark—and in the night a solitary dog is barking, all
the space that stands about us filled with his insistence, night and stars

consumed in that repeated sound, the measure of a cosmos that
descends upon us, taking up the trees in their occasions, then
the sleeping birds, the room where we are lying, all of us in one
regime in which the darkness calls and then is silent: this is our
bed, the dog we thought we heard no more than his appeal against
the silence it evokes, and with us lies the darkened sun, the day
asleep beside us. How can we be more awake than this, awake

beyond the sun, awake inside the solitude that is the pure
inside of all that we approach, the least of stones that we recall
that lay beside our feet when it was light, the silence holding them,
of trees and our eyes, the silence holding everything that we
behold, the silence holding silence rising over us at night—
nothing else endures, the distance of it intimate, a kind
of flesh invisible that keeps us, and the night, the barking dog.

Leaving Morocco

You walked into my eyes. Afterward you found a place where you could feel at home. It happened many years ago, but when we could not say, perhaps at night and unobserved, the only sign the moon suspended in the apple tree that stands beyond our window. Then eternity arrived and slept with us when we would sleep and wake when we would wake. Should one of us begin to speak, eternity would answer if inclined. How else to understand the things we say

that do not seem to have a sense that we might understand, or where do moments of the light come from when all around us darkness sits? You say that we are growing old, the apple tree that we had known seems older too, the many winters it endured now visible upon its branches. What is there to say that moons do not say for us, each of them the same, the harvest that it bears a heaven near enough to touch, remembered moons that seem to fall into the fall?

Place

The words I speak to you do not originate from me, they fall
as leaves would fall, and when I speak, a tree stands up inside my mouth
and in the words an echo of the leaves remains. It is a tree
that opens in the dark, the moon its light, and on its branches birds
come down, their sleeping undisturbed, only their dreams becoming known,
the dreams of solitary birds that rise in consonance with moons,
the leaves, the air invisible around them, dreams of their desires

rising through the stars, the long descents, the nothing that surrounds
them blue and full, the song escaping them a singing O of their
abandon, birds but birds transcendent, falling into flight and nothing
more, remembered by the moon, the light that lies upon the leaves
which are the mind of what I speak, our abandon held in that
forever, its desire spoken, breathing through these little sounds
that I have given you to speak again, eternity alive.

Abandon

It could be said we never spoke. What did I tell you of the stars,
the sadness of the sun at night in dreams, surrounded by the dark,
the silence of the birds? Perhaps you've noticed too that memory
is often like a music never heard before—you enter it
and you are taken up by what could not have happened, rhythms of
a past you never were a part of, its surprises coming down
upon you, sitting in your sight so deep with their familiar look
that they become an aspect of the things that you forget again,

a chair that you have sat upon so often it is almost you,
and you are taken not by music but by something in yourself
that was not known before, or known and never understood, that you
had flowers growing in a place that had been passed but not perceived,
and all the flowers stood together calling what they thought your name
to be, a name that you had never heard but one that was akin
to what the music was. Your face might then surprise yourself to see
the sense the flowers made upon it and the light around it out.

Letter

Before us stood a long alley of trees, behind them winter light
that when it reached them stopped in lines of shadows that extended them
upon the ground, across the snow and into distances that blurred,
impossible to grasp what lay against the end, and all of it—
the sun without its warmth, the trees in rows, the shadows, winter and
the sense of what is endless—it was known before we saw it, and when
it came upon us, we were given us, something that had been inside

us but unknown until the moment that they stood so perfectly before
our eyes that saw them in the fading light until the shade became
the snow, the ordinary air upon us. We were then, and what
we knew was not of trees, it was of knowing, how it is that we
are miracles that rest upon our hands, and when we look again
they are not there, something in us that now is not, a world before
us empty-handed, old eternities that are our shapes and trees.

Miracles

Our shadows stretched across the freshly fallen snow so far it seemed
to reach the near horizon, falling into frozen ponds and rising
to the fields that followed: all that was left was what the moon gave off,
the air as far as we might see largesse of light that filled our eyes,
and breathing through our flesh that stood between the moon and snow, a flesh
of light surrendered. Creatures walking through it were not possible
to see as other than the moon in other guises, and the shadows that

they cast dissolve into themselves across the snow, the lives we thought
were theirs possessing what the moon possesses—nothing final in
their shapes and flowing over in the light with shade that hovers near
the ground impalpable. We must be them, the shades they cast and ours
a breath our bodies exhale, ways of talking then, with no more sound
than snow contains against the ground where we are standing, each of us
a phase of shadow, snow, the moon, our lives not known but otherwise.

Shadowing

Coyotes wake when we lie down upon the verge of sleep enclosed,
intent upon pursuits that take them through the night, always nearby,
the clamour of their sudden laughter rising up beside us. Sleep
does not begin, it enters our bodies unperceived, and then
it is all that we are, a world sleeping in us, desiring nothing
but the sleep we are, the world's only residue within
our flesh the echo of the coyotes and their waking joy where they
are in their midnights, stars rolling through them, stars ablaze upon

their tongues. No other stars rise up inside our nights: we are the sky
without a sun, yet sky that has no sphere of final stars where in
our sleep we might conclude, our prayers hushed against the air, their words
invisible around our bodies. Coyotes lope beneath the sky
at night, its silence on their backs, the quickened folly of their calling
opening the sky, and where it opens we are open, flesh
forgotten with our prayers, the air around the stars flowing through
the sleep we are, so close we are their intimates, breathing fire.

Coyotes

The world lay down before us just as it was spoken first, silence
still upon it, birds not yet about to call to one another,
not a breath of wind, a tree with only silence for its leaves.
How many nights we saw the world so, the moon no older than
the moment when it falls into your eyes, across the snow and on
the near horizon where the barking dogs lie down in silence. Absence
of the merest sound makes us suddenly awake, as one might wake
inside a seed before the seed has settled fully in the ground,

a seed in its conception that contains its cosmos, pregnant and
invisible, the stars in place and yet to move, and each of them
upon the sill of saying *now*, when all that follows leaps into
the air, no move that does not celebrate the stars, no star that does
not celebrate the stroke of its enlightenment: for us there is
nothing to do, to breathe will be enough, the dance that animates
the grass the dance now turning in our now, and there the moon
in us, its rising in our eyes always beginning, still to come.

Silences

Of all of them you are the one who carries forth the sun, a sun
of more than light, or light that when it opens does not fall but gathers
in—a bird that moved against the corner of your eye unseen,
a hand that you remember but without a sense of whose it may
have been, a word that someone spoke and was not heard. It is a light
that stands unseen above the light, the highest tree that rises in
the universe, its leaves around us quiet in the wind, and on
its crown the memory of a bird that was born in fire, the fall

of ashes, then, a lesser light, a shadow that the tree but dimly
bears, yet enough that it is known to be around us kept inside the shade,
remembered in that place where birds of fire are recalled, all light
in flight between infinity and us: you can be nowhere else
but in the light, its opening the movements that possess your hands
a flutter passing through them in the darkest night, impossible
it might be seen, but known, a gesture of the infinite that has
no other way to recollect where you are turning through the fire.

Family

Because you are my breath, the trees I told you of before are not
the trees I thought they were, and when the moon is rising through their branches
it takes shape within the eyes, flowers and appears a lotus
floating where the mind pools, no other thought but thought of it in its
emergence, not a flower but the nakedness of light that when
it opens, is a mind that is the moon, its silence not the loss
of music but the breathing of the air withdrawn, the branches of

the trees attentive, light so deep upon them they cannot be seen
as they had been: it is a world waiting, all its knowledge this
arrival that is mind so still the trees could rise to heaven in
its place, and as they rise, their rising is an offering to you,
the trees that hold the moon, the air above them open to the mute
eternities unseen, the lotus that is what I speak to you
unheard at night, afloat upon your breath, ours the shape it takes.

Lotus

All that stood behind you was the stars, and if the truth were told,
the stories that were said of them was what I saw of light that settled
on your hair, so when I wake at night my hands are full of what
their light casts forth, mythologies instilled in them. Nothing then
is seen of them unless the gods and goddesses recited there
are other than the words and stars that we have known them by, yet they
stand up upon my waiting hands, the air around them burning through

the dark, the fire so pure it feeds upon itself alone, our gaze
upon them taking sight away, our eyes so deep with fire it is
the only air we know, the air that turns around your naked face,
nowhere inside the light to hide. If this is what we are, we are
but children of the fire, and all that we may give it in return
is not our faces nor our hands but our all of nakedness,
without the cover of our words on us, just us as stars.

Transfigured

Certain trees spread their branches nowhere but in the mind, the sky
behind them almost full of early winter evening light, the gathered birds,
the silence of the trees archaic, knowledge overflowing them
and falling through the light, a light without the brilliance of the day
but rising for a moment everywhere, from grass, the hidden stones,
the last cloud, a knowledge that without the slightest motion fills,
and when its fullness has been reached, the silence visible of trees

begins to speak without the sign of alphabets: their branches hold
a universe, that music no one hears but sees, the grasping of
it sudden, light that is a dance that in its fullness does not move,
all its movements already given to the grass, the stone, the cloud,
and in it you are found, the you that is the knowledge trees contain,
and with a sureness that is not in us to wield, they recite what is
everywhere in the air, the farthest cloud revealed, its name bestowed.

Naming

Evening rises from the ground. It moves unseen across the grass,
enlarging stones beyond their measure in the sun until they are
just shadows of themselves, becoming in the greater evening stones
in memory, the evening moving over ground like snow but snow
of darkness rising, settling first upon your feet, their steps about
to disappear into the memories of stones and grass, and as
it rises you discover that the sun was nothing other than

the light that hid from you the way you were to go, and everything
that now takes shape beside you full of its unknownness given up
to you so you can take it in your hands, and in return the stones
as they recall themselves are now where you will find what you you are,
the darkness falling open into you, the edges of the world lost.
Where is the moon if not inside you now, the largest stars, the light
you thought was theirs the light that is your bones, the movement of your feet

as they with evening start to dance into the dark, the ground beneath
but no more present than a memory of grass where you rise up
into the fullness of the dark, and so to be the heaven of
the world, and where it is, the where of what you know, every blade
of grass a whisper of the possible? And there are all your steps—
the rising of the dark, the leaping stones, the knowing of the moon—
nothing not upon you that is not the darkness radiant.

Illumined

All the children rose and walked away as one, each passing through
the eye's horizons never to be seen again. All you could ask
was where they went, the moment they were here as fleeting as the stars
that fade at dawn. We looked again, but what we saw was emptiness,
and it was larger than the sky without the sun, the moon, the stars,
an emptiness that fell, and if its falling could be heard, it would
have been the sound of feet departing, smaller feet and smaller sounds

that were beyond our hearing. If there are any left, they are
with us, and not in what we heard but in the moment after, that
gesture that is impossible to bring again, your hand that lifts
into the air and unaware returns, nothing inside it grasped,
the nothing where they are at home, and when you touched me, nothing fell
across my shoulder, sun and moon and stars settling there, their light
invisible, the sound of steps within the air unheard and clear,

no bird in passing capable of such a music, nothing of
the sun in that refulgence that you carried in your eyes
the night that we had seen a deeper night than those that we
had known, and in that darkness absence given up to us, as one
might hold a hand and in between the pressing palms a space that does
not close. It is the absence that if it were not, then we would not
be holding our hands as we are now, children passing between.

Children

You walked alone into the yard, your eyes untouched by trees. If there
were birds around you where you walked, they were not to be seen, intent
upon their morning prayers, the silence that they keep absolute,
and as you walk, you lean as one who would arrive before arriving,
taking something in without a knowledge of its being what
you might be looking for. Perhaps you are not after anything,
but something that you cannot see has taken you, and you have yielded

to it. Were you to waken now, a world as you had never known
it might surprise you: before the trees took shape again, the breath
of nothing would obscure your gaze, the nothing you had stumbled on,
the trees invisible, the absent birds not absent, but an absence
in itself where you had stepped, the world open, moons beneath
your floating feet instead of grass and earth. The slightest breeze
might settle in your mind forever, leaves falling slowly past.

Yard

No matter what the pace my walking takes, the picket fence that stands
along my way is always there, a patient, little fence that marks
the boundary of a yard I do not know, and at its base a line
of grass is growing, high and brown and almost always just above
the snow. I cannot say if anyone is living in the house,
all the windows curtained. I imagine it as of the final
things that one might see before the light is spent, a fence with grass

that no one thinks to take away, and stillness in the air behind
it where, if apples were to fall, they would escape into the air
before they reached the ground. The shapes of children, such as you or me,
have walked beneath them unconcerned, the trace of disappearances
not in their sight, and they are waving as I pass, but not at me
nor at each other, they are waving at the air, the moon, the fall
of apples. Anything that we might take as absence they have it

in full possession of the moment, passage in its fullness in
their hands: so I have thought to see you as you may have been, a fence
between the times where we have passed, the child that you were a place
that you return to in your stories. Laughter sometimes rises from
behind the fence. I look and there is nothing there but naked air,
perhaps a leaf the wind has yet to pick, the only knowledge that
we have that we were there the grass that waits for apples and the moon.

Fence

Since the moment you began to contemplate the light, the edges
of the alphabet were at your fingertips, the alpha where
it all began and the omega where it ended, in between
letters pell-mell that leaped and danced into the world that rose up
into your mouth, but alphas were not common there, the letters were
more indistinct and unconcerned with primal order, forming on
the air upon your lips and floating off into the summer nights,

flowers of words that were the clear anthologies of what you said
and left unsaid, the letters intertwined for moments, then apart,
the matter they brought forth enough to change the air as if the trees
had been beside you more majestic than it would have been if they
were seen, their branches hanging over us with fruit so tender we
could not prevent our hands from reaching upward, past them into stars,
the heaven that we grasped a heaven that was ours, the turning of

the moon a knowledge intimate as breath, the one omega that
was given us the sphere that it described, the O where our hands began
an O without the certainty of other alphabets, the letters it
contained a moon that has no spelling we possess, a moon that if
we spoke it would become a moon that we had not perceived before,
its sphere grown larger, and the night of its beginning night without
the letters that we thought enough, the night before the nights began.

Alphabet

If anything, you feel a kinship with the birds that hover near
your house, early in the spring and when the autumn comes, but not
the birds, only the moments of their coming and their going in
the air. In some eternity a river flows away not far
from where you live: it rises where the light might rise, descending into
threads of evening, each of them a shade of night, and each
reflecting something held in memory and the other side of light,

a river that is flowing slowly through you, distance falling through
your hands. Time is unknown to you, only the passage of the light,
certain shadows that possess an anonymity that brings them so
near you might say that this is what the birds would mean suspended in
your eyes, a change of air and music in a sudden shower, notes
that are a light that leaps from light, and when they cease, shadows hang
unmoving in the air, each one of other memories of light.

Visit

Snow was falling from acacia trees: it was the spring that fell
and silence and the and of everything that falls, the space between
the branches and the ground the only space where nothing and the stars
fall without ever reaching earth. How close to tears the trees appear
to be, their beauty given up but given to another beauty
where desires that might take their residence in us have no
way in. All the beauty of the world is so: its beauty is

never what seems to fall as snow, the playful stars, their passage on
your face, the look that follows petals floating farther through the air,
the knowledge that the air we think we see is all the air there is—
how to go on, to be the passing of all things that pass, that
is beauty, and the you you are suddenly filled with all the falling
of the air, no other beauty given us but this in its
arrival, instants of whatever you were now, you and silence and

Other Acacias

Nothing can explain the sun, or grass, or children passing in
the street, and when they're gone, all that remains of them is laughter hanging
in the air. If reason avails, it avails as a crown
of clover freshly mown and woven in your hair, where children
in their summers played, the colour of the clover children's laughter.
What is the keeping, then, of all—not children but their passing by,
the days we think the sun in movement up and down, the places where

they are, or—unforgotten—laughter hidden in the air, the air
immortal, every sudden peal of it an echo of a primal
laughter, and there the sun, clover and a summer? If we are,
we are the sun wherever it is in the air, the laughter that
we heard, the sun in passing, a beginning that returns, the day
we thought was gone, not gone but settled in the clover circling
your hair, impossible to say what light is in the sky and there.

Laughter

OTHER BOOKS OF POETRY
Published by the University of Alberta Press

Apostrophes II: through you I
E.D. Blodgett
0–88864–304–7
$14.95 paper

**Apostrophes IV:
speaking you is holiness**
E.D. Blodgett
0–88864–352–7
$16.95 paper

An Ark of Koans
E.D. Blodgett
Jacques Brault, Illustrator
0–88864–404–3
$19.95 paper

The Snowbird Poems
Robert Kroetsch
0–88864–426–4
$24.95 paper

The Hornbooks of Rita K
Robert Kroetsch
0–88864–372–1
$16.95 paper

Bloody Jack
Dennis Cooley
Douglas Barbour, Introduction
0–88864–391–8
$19.95 paper